ANIMALS *in* DANGER

Whooping Crane

Rod Theodorou

Heinemann Library
Chicago, Illinois

Designed by Ron Kamen
Illustrations by Dewi Morris/Robert Sydenham
Originated by Ambassador Litho Ltd.
Printed and bound in Hong Kong/China

05 04 03 02 01
10 9 8 7 6 5 4 3 2 1

Library of Congress Cataloging-in-Publication Data
Theodorou, Rod.
    Whooping crane / Rod Theodorou.
       p. cm. -- (Animals in danger)
    Includes bibliographical references and index (p.).
    ISBN 1-57572-274-7 (library)
     1. Whooping crane--Juvenile literature. 2. Endangered species--Juvenile literature. [1.
Whooping crane. 2. Cranes (Birds) 3. Endangered species.] I. Title.

QL696.G84 T44 2001
598.3'2--dc21

00-063263

Acknowledgments
The author and publishers are grateful to the following for permission to reproduce copyright
material: Ardea,p. 4; Associated Press, p. 25; Bat Conservation International/Merlin D. Tuttle, p. 4;
BBC/Thomas D. Mangelsen, p. 16; BBC/Lynn M. Stone, pp. 5, 7, 8, 12, 20; BBC/Doug Bengeton, p.
14; Bruce Coleman/Jeff Foott, p. 17; Bruce Coleman/John Shaw, p. 4; DRK Photo/Jeff Foott, p. 9;
FLPA, p. 22; FLPA/Robin Chittenden, p. 6; Natural Science Photos/Ken Cole, pp. 15, 19, 26; Oxford
Scientific Films/Judd Cooney, p. 21; Still Pictures/Thomas D. Mangelsen, p. 18; The Stock Market,
p. 24; Davis Thompson, p. 27; Wood Buffalo, p. 23; WWF Photolibrary, p. 11.

Cover photograph reproduced with permission of BBC Natural History Library.

Every effort has been made to contact copyright holders of any material reproduced in this book.
Any omissions will be rectified in subsequent printings if notice is given to the publisher.

Some words are shown in bold, **like this.** You can
find out what they mean by looking in the glossary.

Contents

Animals in Danger

leatherback sea turtle

gray bat

koala

All over the world, more than 25,000 animal **species** are in danger. Some are in danger because their homes are being destroyed. Many are in danger because people hunt them.

4

This book is about whooping cranes and why they are **endangered**. Unless people protect them, whooping cranes will become **extinct**. We will only be able to find out about them from books like this.

What Are Whooping Cranes?

Whooping cranes are birds. They are the tallest birds in North America. A **male** whooping crane is as tall as a person and has a **wingspan** as long as a person is tall.

Whooping cranes are named after their loud call, which sounds like a trumpet being blown. They are shy birds that are easily disturbed.

What Do Whooping Cranes Look Like?

Whooping cranes have a long neck and very long legs. They have a small head with red skin on the face. They also have a long, strong **bill**.

Adult whooping cranes are white with black feathers on their wing tips. Young whooping cranes are reddish-brown.

Where Do Whooping Cranes Live?

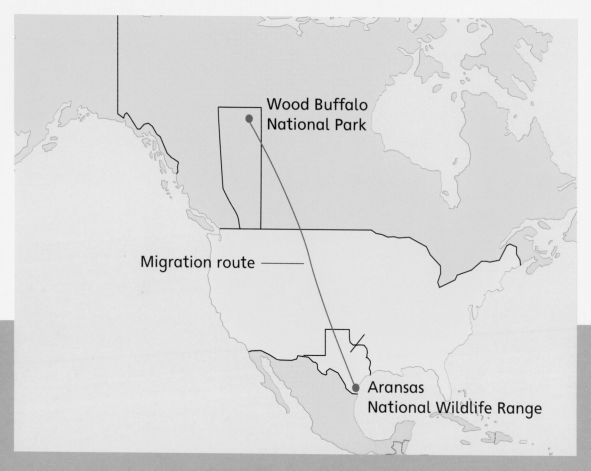

Wood Buffalo National Park

Migration route —

Aransas National Wildlife Range

Whooping cranes live in Canada for half of the year. Every year they **migrate** to spend the winter in the U. They stay in the warm water of the Gulf of Mexico.

Whooping cranes are **wetland** birds. They need to live in places where there is plenty of shallow water. Here they can find their food and be safe from **predators**.

What Do Whooping Cranes Eat?

Whooping cranes are **omnivores**. They stand in shallow water and use their long necks and **bills** to spear their food. They eat snails, crabs, water insects, frogs, and **minnows.**

Whooping cranes will eat snakes and small **rodents** if they can catch them. They also eat berries and other wild fruit.

Whooping Crane Chicks

Male and **female** whooping cranes **mate** for life.
The female lays two eggs in the spring. Both
parents take turns sitting on the eggs to keep
them warm.

The eggs hatch at different times. The oldest chick pecks at the younger chick and tries to push it out of the nest. The younger chick usually dies.

Migration

After about 80 days the chicks have learned to fly. Around mid-September the family flies off on the long journey south to Texas.

On the way the whooping cranes stop to rest and eat. They arrive at the Gulf Coast of Texas between late October and mid-November.

Unusual Whooping Crane Facts

When they **migrate,** whooping cranes travel an amazing 2,500 miles! They use their huge wings to **glide** on the high winds. They can stay in the air for hours longer than you are in school each day.

Whooping cranes are very shy. If their breeding grounds are disturbed too much they may fly away and not lay any eggs that year.

How Many Whooping Cranes Are There?

Over 100 years ago there may have been about 2,100 whooping cranes in the world. They lived from the Arctic coast down to central Mexico.

By 1940 this number had dropped to less than 20! The whooping crane was nearly **extinct**. Now there are about 400 whooping cranes. More than 100 of them live in **captivity**.

Why Is the Whooping Crane in Danger?

Whooping cranes need waterways and **wetlands** to live in. During the last 100 years many of these wetlands have been destroyed to make room for farms, roads, and cities.

As more people have spread across Canada and the U.S., whooping cranes have been hunted and their eggs have been stolen by collectors.

Many cranes die when they fly into electrical power lines. Some of these power lines are on the whooping cranes' **migration** route.

Whooping cranes spend their winter hunting
around the Gulf Coast of Texas. Oil spills
and other pollution from ships have killed
many cranes.

How Is the Whooping Crane Being Helped?

Canada and the United States of America have passed laws to **protect** the whooping crane. Hunting, stealing eggs, or disturbing their nests is now illegal.

26

Some whooping cranes have been caught and put in places where they can be protected. Their numbers have increased, but the cranes are still close to becoming **extinct**.

Whooping Crane Fact File

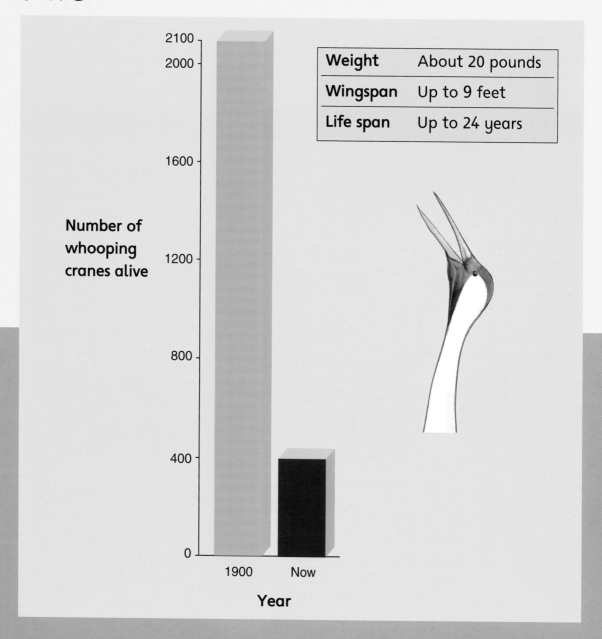

Weight	About 20 pounds
Wingspan	Up to 9 feet
Life span	Up to 24 years

Number of whooping cranes alive

Year

2100
2000

1600

1200

800

400

0

1900   Now

28

World Danger Table

	Number when animal was listed as endangered	Number that may be alive today
Whooping Crane	less than 20	about 400
Bald Eagle	about 500	about 4,200
California Condor	about 20	about 56
Great Blue Heron	The great blue heron is not **endangered.**	about 10,000
Peregrine Falcon	about 600	about 3,500

There are many other birds in the world that need to be protected so they won't become **extinct.** This table shows some of these birds.

How Can You Help the Whooping Crane?

If you and your friends raise money for the whooping crane, you can send it to these organizations. They take the money and use it to pay conservation workers and to buy food and tools to help save the whooping crane.

Defenders of Wildlife
1101 Fourteenth St., N.W. #1400
Washington, DC 20005

Whooping Crane Conservation Association
1393 Henderson Highway
Breaux Bridge, LA 70517

World Wildlife Fund
1250 Twenty-fourth St.
P.O. Box 97180
Washington, DC 20037

More Books to Read

Dutemple, Lesley A. *North American Cranes.* Minneapolis, Minn.: Lerner Publishing Group, 1998. An older reader can help you with this book.

Parker, Janice, and Karen Dudley. *Whooping Cranes.* Austin, Tex.: Raintree Steck-Vaughn, 1997. An older reader can help you with this book.

Roop, Peter, and Connie Roop. *Seasons of the Cranes.* New York: Walker and Company, 1989. An older reader can help you with this book.

Glossary

bill	beak of a bird
captivity	kept by people and not living free in the wild
endangered	group of animals that is dying out, so there are few left
extinct	group of animals that has died out and can never live again
female	girl or woman
glide	to go down slowly and smoothly
male	boy or man
mate	when a male and a female come together to have babies
migrate	to move from one place to another, often in spring and fall
minnow	small, silvery fish
omnivore	animal that eats both plants and animals
predator	animal that hunts and kills other animals
protect	to keep safe
rodents	small animals such as mice, squirrels, rats, and beavers
species	group of similar animals
wetland	land that is covered with, or often flooded by, water
wingspan	length of a bird's outstretched wings measured from wing tip to wing tip

Index